LIFE COACHING DECODED

☐ **How To Achieve Extraordinary Results**
☐ **Earn +6 Figures As A Professional Life Coach**

PaTrisha-Anne Todd

Sponsored by
CoachingLeadsToSuccess.com

Table of Contents

LETTER FROM PATRISHA-ANNE

Dear student of life coaching or new life coach,

Life coaching is a gift, and I am delighted that you showed up and stepped up to purchase a copy of my book 'Life Coaching Decoded', I know it will help you to clarify exactly what life coaching is and how it can transform negative thinking into positive forward moving thinking. Discover how with the correct steps it's possible to powerfully create a better more compelling and stronger bigger change in your life by adopting a positive mental attitude to understand why you want a particular goal. Uncover the know how to form positive forward moving new habits resulting in the best way you can achieve your goal quickly, with ease and then help your clients get their desired results!

If you are looking to live your best life and willing to practice a wonderful occupation that creates a well-rounded and happy work life balance then life coaching is for you as it will enhance your ideas, it will impact your thinking, improve your time management so you work smarter not harder and escape the 9-5 grind. Life coaching will influence positively and profoundly as you steadily elevate both your lifestyle and coach your clients who are ready to change their current status quo especially during these difficult times to achieve an all-round level of life and work balance. If it's your aim to become a professional life coach, then this book will answer the most crucial questions you have and will help you understand the key principles involved in effective life coaching and find the best way to become a professional life coach ensuring you make an impact on clients as you coach them to create a transformation in their life while you earn a substantial income.

I believe I can help you master the craft of professional life coaching so that in the first instance you uplevel your lifestyle, transforming your life for the better giving you more time freedom, ease to work, opportunity to experience abundance, optimal health, wonderful relationships and joy while you build a life coaching business you love delivering quality coaching to clients who are hungry for your style of coaching.

Read the book and gain insights into the craft of professional life coaching. You can send me a message with any questions you may have, I am here to help and answer questions that can lead to you finding your brilliance and becoming the best life coach you can be in your chosen business niche.

Yours in Coaching,
PaTrisha-Anne Todd

"Today is preparation for the next opportunity"

Quote from 'Pepper Your Life with Dreams'

INTRODUCTION TO LIFE COACHING DECODED

Questions and answers on the craft of professional life coaching.

* * * * *

Congratulations on taking the first step towards busting those myths that have caused confusion about becoming a professional life coach and replacing them with the truth to some very profound questions. I am thrilled that you are reading my book 'Life Coaching Decoded'.

I decided to put pen to paper, or should I say - let my fingers loose on the keyboard of the computer and write this book to answer the most common questions that people have asked me over the previous +five decades since I began coaching clients from all walks of life worldwide. Some were pursuing a career with a corporate looking to climb the corporate ladder, some were ready to ditch the job and work for themselves. Others were already small business owners offering a whole range of services and products, keen to turn their inner dreams of helping others with the idea of offering professional life coaching services. Those clients wanted to turn their ideas into a reality, and coach. Perhaps you too are a likeminded soul who is curious and wants to know more about how to have a fulfilling and prosperous career as a professional life coach. Keep reading as I unlock the secrets to your questions so you too can experience success as a professional life coach. The answers are waiting for you.

Your questions will be answered as you read and digest the responses given. You hold in your hands either the physical book or electronic version on your reading device, 'Life Coaching Decoded', now read the words. You'll see organised and all-encompassing truths on the topic of life coaching, the possible struggles and of course the wins. It's my intention that you discover how to navigate your way through the questions that are important to you, and how best you can earn money providing professional life coaching services to clients who are eager to be coached by you.

The six foundational questions to consider before deciding to practice as a professional life coach.

1. "How can I coach professionally?"

2. "Can I make money as a life coach?"

3. "What skills do I need to coach and not become overwhelmed myself?"

4. "Do I work part-time or full-time as a life coach?"

5. "Which certification do I need to coach?"

6. "Is life coaching a real job?"

The answers to those fundamental six questions will confirm what you are thinking and give you a true understanding of what life coaching is and how it can transform your lifestyle when applied correctly to a satisfying career as a professional life coach. So, you can stop wondering what is really meant by life coaching, the skills and tools required to deliver professional life coaching for a successful outcome and if being certified to work as a life coach is a legal requirement!

I am truly honoured to share with you the +five decades in the study of personal development, metaphysics, NLP (neuro linguistic programming), and practical experience of life coaching I've acquired. Now, you too can begin living life on purpose, feel fulfilled and live life by design. As you read, you'll realise that this book is different and if you take the core principles and essence of its content to heart, you'll automatically begin to make a difference in your life and the lives of others you encounter. I want to lay the foundation of how you can have a prosperous and meaningful business, how to know what you want and focus on achieving your heart's desire. Also, how to gain a solid grasp of the principles and practice of professional life coaching as a personal development tool that can bring about positive transformation to the lives of individuals who choose to become a better version of themselves. It's possible to create an extraordinary lifestyle, to experience a deep and meaningful transformation by unlocking your passion to help others while you create a business providing security and wealth for you and your family. With confidence you can say goodbye to the 'rat race'.

Keep reading to gain valuable insights of practical coaching procedures that ensure you coach as a professional, business strategies and tips to absorb on effective communication and making a living either full or part time as a life coach.

Did you know that there are across-the-board techniques you can use to ensure you stay on track as you move towards your goals. Simple tracking practices and skills to adopt for enriching your inner core belief system. There are untruths to correct aimed specifically at *wannabe, new life coaches* and even *operational life coaches* who do not know how to easily proceed forward to achieving a better positive and fast result.

Drawing on my experience and extensive knowledge of personal development, NLP, metaphysics and life coaching I answer within the pages of 'Life Coaching Decoded' the repeatedly asked, foundational questions and more! I will help you discover in a succinct and direct spirit what professional life coaching is and most importantly what it is not, particularly if you intend to follow through and set up a life coaching business that can bring you a more than nominal return on your investment. I will help you unlock your potential to become an exceptional life coach and learn the necessary tools to start and grow a life coaching business that aligns with your passion, purpose, your core belief system and most importantly the goals you hold in your heart to make an impact while living your own dream life.

Just by the simple action of reading this book you have already stoked your curiosity factor in how best to master the craft of professional life coaching. You've probably been told by others how you'd make a great life coach because you have a great way of listening, even giving advice, or just by the fact that you enjoy helping others and want to help them gain the advantage while you reap the rewards of building a successful business that attracts an endless stream of ideal clients to coach as you build and enjoy a compelling lifestyle of your own.

It's important to know that life coaching is a competitive profession, but with the correct tools and dedication to the craft, the work is rewarding, positively transformative and lucrative for those who are prepared to become uncomfortable with their status quo and seriously want to align their passions and values to the technique of forward moving thinking and taking the necessary action to achieve the goal of becoming a professional life coach.

Welcome… all things that will help you expand and claim success.

Quote from 'Pepper Your Life with Dreams'

STEP INTO YOUR PASSION AND MAKE A DIFFERENCE

Question – What is life coaching?

Answer – It's a wide-ranging question, as it leads into so much more when looked at correctly. Life coaching is a huge part of the tool of personal development to develop self-growth in a specific area of focus. It's a tool to learn and progress how to take actionable steps to expand and grow a person's awareness and set positive forward moving goals along with creating momentum and on-going motivation.

Over the years a lot of people including wannabe life coaches and prospective coaching clients have asked me 'What exactly is life coaching and truly, can life coaching help me sort out a problem or gain the advantage in my business and make money?"

There is no secret to the concept of life coaching because basically it's a vehicle to achieve something. It's a growth and personal development tool that helps the individual get clear on what they really want and allows them to align their thoughts and energy to move away from those negative beliefs which hold them back and to find how best to turn dreams into reality. In other words, life coaching is a step-by-step tool to participate in pinpointing the desired goal, in other words getting clear on what that goal is regardless of the area the challenge is located, be that a challenge of business building, of finding optimal health, enjoying special relationships, exploring spiritual growth, adjusting, and securing time and money freedom. When it comes to life coaching it's possible to optimise the route to achieving any goal – Just to be clear, I mean _any goal!_

Of course, the goal needs to be ethical and legal, that goes without saying and another 'of course' point to keep at front of mind, is that the goal is always the goal of the client. By that I mean it is not a pre-determined goal set by another, such as an eager parent for a child, a spouse, the boss even the aspirations of a teacher. Goals have to belong to the person who is prepared to reach out and achieve that goal, not a person who doesn't want to engage in goal achievement, or a complaining employee, a reluctant student, or a stubborn child. All will become clear as you continue to read.

Knowing what the goal is and why it's desired is important to recognise and understand as there is a secret in the way life coaching is delivered. I talk about this 'secret' within the book. First though, it's necessary to de-mystify the concept of life coaching.

WHEN CAN I CALL MYSELF A LIFE COACH?

Once you have the framework of your life coaching business in place, (a business plan will give you the direction of your life coaching business, along with detailed steps and procedures to take to set up the coaching contracts, NDA, non-disclosure agreement, sessions and pricing to ensure you run your life coaching business successfully from the get-go), and can competently use the coaching model to work with clients to have them achieve positive forward moving results, you can refer to yourself as a life coach. My recommendation for the fastest results driven coaching model is the '*6 Step Coaching Model*'. This tool gives instant results and allows you as the life coach to deploy best coaching practices in terms of confidentiality, process and results.

ENVISION THE VISION

Professional life coaches use a specific methodology, a growth tool to help clients dig deep into their brain box and recognise their inherent knowledge and wisdom. This process will uncover their true desires, values, priorities and identify exactly what they want, then help them to clarify how best to set manageable, yet big goals, sometimes big audacious scary goals, and to progress towards the set goal with what they have from where they are by determining the most effective path to achieving their goals. This is professional life coaching a powerful catalyst to transformation. It's all about recognising what they know, of dreaming big, of visualising their ideal future and developing the correct action plan starting from where they are using what they have and taking consistent positive forward moving action, one step at a time which fully supports personal empowerment as clients take charge of their own life journey with daily consistent action in a timely fashion and by that, I mean daily forward moving steps to the goal.

It's interesting to see how growth happens. I just love to work with clients who are itching to experience a transformation from the lifestyle they are currently living to a more satisfying and fulfilled life. I feel emotional when I watch clients make incremental progress and clarify piece by piece what it is they want, their objectives in life, their desired relationships, their financial investments, their health, their all-round better management of their lifestyle and pivot from someone who was confused about their future, worried about how they could find the time to work on their goals and even dig into their finances to invest in their personal growth. It's a very special kind of satisfaction that comes from seeing clients flourish and enhance their overall lifestyle and reach their next level of fulfilment factor.

IS LIFE COACHING JUST A WAY OF TELLING PEOPLE HOW TO LIVE THEIR LIFE?

NO, is the answer.

As professional life coaches we do not tell a client how to live their life or give them the answer to questions that would mean them making a decision that might be detrimental to their overall well-being. Telling someone how to live their life is not ethical nor wise to offer direction in a situation that might lead to loss and unhappiness. Life coaching is an open relationship between the coach and the client who is ready to *s-t-r-e-t-c-h* their comfort zone and take action towards changing their sauts quo. A life coach is a catalyst to draw out of the coachee their personal and professional dreams and goals. With quality open ended questions the life coach will facilitate a stunning transformation of them unlocking their mind to becoming the best they can be. The coachee's potential will be released to the highest level and unfathomable success set in motion.

True life coaching is a partnership between the client and life coach who uses a life coaching model to purposefully step by step move the client forward towards their desired goal. Life coaching is the association of scientific vibrational frequency and going after goals that align to that frequency.

WHEN PEOPLE SAY "YOU SHOULD BE A LIFE COACH"

Oftentimes someone will tell another that they should consider becoming a life coach. This might have happened to you. A friend, colleague or a family member might have told you that *"You are such a good listener, you should be a life coach"*, or *"You always know what to say and give good advice, you should be a life coach"*.

But neither of these qualities alone lend themselves to quality life coaching. You see being a good listener and speaking with a client is only part of the process.

The fundamental part of life coaching is – listening to the client's response to specific quality open ended questions you'll be asking. I've mentioned this before, it's a growth tool that allows the client to open their mind and imagine what life could look like if they adopted new forward moving habits to accomplish their goals.

Life coaching in not advice giving such as you'd find within the scope of a career's advisor or a financial advisor or is it consulting when a person is hired to trouble shoot a situation, usually within a corporation and layout a plan of action to reach a specific goal. There are also medical consultants in the medical field who work one on one with patients who seek medical advice to regain health.

Business coaching, cosmic soul coaching*, health coaching even sports coaching are industry specific – they are not life coaching!

*The Cosmic Soul Coaching Certification is available at the hub @ CoachingLeadsToSuccess.com

Mentoring is when the mentor explains how they arrived at their goal and goes on to explain to the mentee the steps they took to achieve what they have up until now, maybe even telling of the outcomes that were not so good, while the job of teaching is sharing knowledge to a pupil, and holistic therapy is when the therapist talks and asks questions to bring the client back to the situation leading to where they find themselves now, a process of re-living the negative or a therapeutic hands on session to relieve muscle pain which again is not part of the life coaching experience, and then we have counselling psychology when the counsellor tells a client/patient which course of action to take after asking pertinent questions. All these modalities are not part of the role of a life coach. Each of these professions offer specific treatments to the pupil, client, or patient which a professional life coach will know to recognise in a prospective coaching client and when needed refer on to a specialist practitioner.

There are nuances within the arena of life coaching that come into play when a client seeks the expertise of a life coach to help them make changes to their current lifestyle. This is why a professional life coach's skillset and belief in the power of PMA (positive mental attitude) allows them to work with discerning clients who are ready for change. Life coaching is a sought after personal development tool that makes a positive difference.

A life coach always keeps client confidentiality however should there be an instance of legality a proficient life coach will know if a legal authority be alerted to the person/situation - if a course of action needs to be taken.

*****

All in all, over the years I have personally found life coaching to be a wonderful occupation meeting interesting people, to earn a living giving me time and money freedom. To share via my books and courses. To be featured on international media. To travel the world giving talks on the topic of life coaching and having the privilege of working with curious folk ready to transform their current lifestyles for something better. I have also worked with VIP clients including royalty and entertainment personalities – this too is all available to you.

Congratulate Yourself When You Know You Deserve It

Quote from 'Pepper Your Life with Dreams'

ALIGN LIFE COACHING TO YOUR CORE BELIEF SYSTEM

Question – What is my core belief system and what has it got to do with life coaching?

Answer – Your core belief system is what you are made of, what you think about and believe to be true. It's what makes you tick!

Aligning your spirit and core belief system with life coaching is a unique skillset and one anyone can tap into and achieve with a little guidance and practice.

Wanting to make an impact and difference in the world is something not everyone desires to do or can indeed do. Let me explain.

Since the late 1970's when I first began to practice as a life coach and train individuals to become professional life coaches using my unique '6 Step Coaching Model', I learned the 'why' people want to set up and practice in their own life coaching business.

Basically, life coaching is an extension of PMA, positive mental attitude thinking and doing, and personal development for growth on a personal level and in business, giving opportunity to make a meaningful difference in their own lives and the lives of others.

Adopting the tools of the trade, in this case the '6 Step Coaching Model' which I created and have trained novice life coaches to use with their clients. The 6SCM will,

- ☐ unlock human potential for the user and then give juice to help others
- ☐ to bust through negative beliefs
- ☐ to practice new and positive forward moving habits
- ☐ to overcome obstacles and roadblocks thereby creating a pathway to move forward positively to setting and achieving goals.

This type of work is incredibly fulfilling as it enables individuals who choose to become life coaches connect with people from across the globe in all walks of life and assist them in transforming their lives. Life coaching has become a highly competitive style of work that does not require a legal certification to practice, only the certification of life coaches who wish to become licensed to use specific coaching tools, such as the '6 Step Coaching Model'.

On-going study in the mastery of personal development and business tactics and strategies are part of the cycle of becoming an independent life coach. Of course, the idea of living a balanced life and work existence is an automatic benefit of being in service as a life coach especially within your own business. I can speak from experience as this is exactly how I have lived and worked as a single parent of three.

However, I will say and encourage you to carry out due diligence for any life coaching training you intend to pursue, and consideration must be given to the financial cost and time allocation of such life coach training. Only you as the trainee life coach or new life coach can commit to continual professional development and decide which style of training you prefer to follow through with. As I have mentioned before, life coach training does not require government certification.

Sometimes a license to use a specific life coaching model is offered by the creators of life coaching models, tools along with a training in how to set up a life coaching business. Also, there are private corporations who provide and claim 'industry standards and levels to monitor life coaches'. This is currently not a legal requirement to practice as a life coach.

So, if life coaching is something you would like to do then my recommendation to you is to research the styles of life coaching offered, the models to achieve positive forward moving results and the time and costs involved.

MINDSET

I've talked about PMA (positive mental attitude) which is most definitely a requirement to quality life coaching, as well as study and application to personal success. You see PMA trains the mind to think in positive forward moving patterns.

To envision the vision is part of the mindset training I practice each and every day. I am a firm believer in the *opportunity* of turning the impossible into the *possible*, then creating a *probable* result and finally *predicting* the outcome. It's all about *OPPP*!

Years ago, my first coach asked me what I wanted. At the time it was a question of money, I needed money to purchase a home for my children and me, a place of our own where the children and I could live and thrive. He listened to what I had to say, even the excuses I gave him of why it just wasn't possible to move right now, which by the way I didn't recognise at the time were excuses, to me it was just how it was. Then mid flow he interrupted me and asked me again "what did I want?". I felt a little put out that he had interrupted me when I had been pouring out my heart as to why things were not working out in my life and the difficulties involved in being a single parent while also dealing with health mobility issues. But I stopped talking and thought a while about what he had asked, in fact he had asked me twice what I wanted and this time I answered him with what I really wanted. I told him why such a move was important for me and my family and mentioned the exact amount of money needed for a house move. I also told him that I could 'see' the children and I living this dream as a family.

When I had answered him, he smiled and told me that now I knew why I needed it and exactly how much money was involved, all I had to do was to determine what actions I could take in my current circumstances to raise the cash and get the deed done. All that mattered was 'why' I wanted the money and to recognise what assets I had, which skills and talents I could utilise to achieve the financial amount needed. *Opportunity* had knocked at my door. [OPPP].

What this man told me made sense. OK, so at the time it was challenging but oh my goodness it was worth the thinking and effort

I actually put into accomplishing my heart's desire at that time.

Today I continue to use this style of question and thinking to clarify what I want, to recognise what I know and help me envision the vision. I share this technique with my life coaching students and clients. This is true life coaching!

Challenges Help You Develop Your Character

Quote from 'Pepper Your Life with Dreams'

WORKING WITH YOUR IDEAL CLIENT

Question – I intend to coach anyone and everyone who wants to be coached, so I don't need to know about ideal clients, right?

Answer – No, you'll find that it is impossible to work with any and everyone because the time factor is important to observe. Also, problems will arise, your health, family that will stifle your coaching ambition and may even leave you out of pocket as there are people who would expect you to coach them discounted or free of charge.

Knowing who your ideal client will be for the life coaching service you intend to offer is a critical part in respect of your marketing, your business building, your own work life balance and of course the bottom line. After all, if you don't know who to market to and attract and focus on, you'll not be able to work efficiently, productively and very quickly you'll find you will not be working with ideal clients who understand and appreciate your style of life coaching, or indeed you may not have any clients at all.

What you need to consider are five key factors in order to attract and work with clients who want to work with you, who are aligned with your style of coaching, who trust you to coach them forward and of course to pay the fee you ask.

First [1], what are your prospective clients *pain points*? You need to know this as it will guide you to ascertain if they understand what you can do for them.

Next [2], it's all about the *focus* and their commitment to wanting to change their current status quo. Have they got the work ethic to make changes and take on new habits to give them more of what they want.

From the next pain point you'll discover and become aware of the character of your ideal client. You'll check in with their dreams [3], because you both need to know if they are clear on what they want and know their true desires in life? This is all about their passion in life and the knowing scenario if they had the opportunity to playout the 'what if' question.

What challenges [4] are there in their current circumstances that prevents them from reaching their goal and what are these roadblocks they encounter along the way. Do they know their assets, their net worth, the level at which they can utilise their skills and talents? These are deep questions that you need to know if they know at what level they are playing at.

Then finally [5] it's all about the outcomes, the results they want. Are they able to become emotionally connected to the desired outcome. It's a simple question that is profound.

All five points [1,2,3,4,5] are key factors and will give you the boundaries you can work with and of course help you determine if you want to work only with certain age groups, gender, occupation, career levels and income status. I mention this here as not everyone will be your ideal client. You need to understand your 'who' so you can zone in on these people and communicate professionally with them and set up those boundaries I mentioned earlier for you so, you can deliver quality life coaching.

Determining who your ideal life coaching clients are requires pre-work on your side. In a nutshell you will need to look at the following.

- The niche market you will be working in.
- The demographic and psychographic factors.

Life coaching is your opportunity to support the ideal client and the time you spend on finding out who your ideal client is, is something very special because you will enable them to begin living the life of their dreams and of course you will automatically be living your life by design.

* * * * *

Every Day Is An Opportunity To Make Your Lifestyle New Again

You are not your parents, nor are you anyone else. You are your own person with thoughts and dreams of your own. With the dawn of each day choose to harness the opportunity it brings and make your lifestyle new again.

Quote from 'Pepper Your Life with Dreams'

MONEY TALK

Question – I don't know what to charge?

Answer – As a professional life coach you'll be able to ask for a fair fee for your life coaching service.

Working for yourself is something that many life coaches accomplish relatively quickly, working with clients that brings a lot of joy as well as financial rewards.

Of course, your results and how much you earn depends first on your mindset and then on the format you offer clients which will depend on your personal goals for your business. Included with those two elements will be the level of commitment you take to run your business and how you'll breakthrough any challenges that could cause a setback along the way.

Those goals structured around the niche market you'll work with, the hours you'll make available to clients, whether in person coaching, as a telephone appointment or via a computer software programme. Keep in mind to, if you'll be coaching one-on-one clients, perhaps because of their work schedule, or their personality aligns better to one-on-one coaching which in of itself allows you to work closely with the client and if necessary, adapt a session to meet the individuals' specific needs at that moment in time. Then alternatively coaching multiple clients as a group can tap into the power of a mastermind session utilising the experience of each group member and take the group in the direction you want the coaching to land. Both delivery styles have the potential to provide powerful accountability, client connection and financially bring in multiple higher income amounts.

Another component is if, and when you'll scale the business or sell to exit the business, but either choice you'll have systems in place to facilitate the growth or transfer. All of these factors would have been decided on when you drew up your initial business plan with objectives and goals in mind that you felt were worthy of you and fitting for your brand new life coaching business. By the way, nothing is set in stone and the beauty of working for yourself is the flexibility you have to re-arrange any part of your business plan, just keep in mind that you always need to coach effectively and give value.

Now is the best time to make the decision to become a professional life coach, when you do, you'll automatically begin to change the trajectory of your life for the better, and as you learn to assist others to make their own transformation and earn income that you can scale.

The only thing you need to do is decide the style of training you'd like to invest in, but while you are thinking about that I recommend you get yourself a copy of my book the '6 Step Coaching Model', read it, digest the words, and begin to use the 6SCM* for yourself in your daily life – yes, in your daily life be that organising your business or carrying out personal tasks. Give it a try it will help you to clarify what you want and need to do. You'll be amazed at the results you'll achieve, quickly and with ease.

With determination in your heart go for the goal and see how much you prosper along the way.

Quote from 'Pepper Your Life with Dreams'

*THE 6SCM

The 6SCM is a key tool that organises thinking, paving the way for success. This tool will improve how you think and revolutionise your coaching that repeatedly provides a satisfying and lucrative lifestyle. Apply the 6SCM to any coaching situation and watch the solution magically appear!

Professional Life Coach training using the 6SCM. Visit @ CoachingLeadsToSuccess.com

DAY DREAMING WORKS AND YOU'LL LOVE IT

Question – isn't day dreaming just for people who have missed the boat and can't get ahead in their job or life in general?

Answer – No, day dreaming is an important part of character building and is a tool that life coaches use to support their clients tap into their Reticular Activating System the part of the brain that filters the thoughts and helps 'day-dreamers' choose what to focus on.

There are strategies and tactics for every conceivable situation and professional life coaching also has its strategies and tactics.

So, at the beginning of this book you read what life coaching is and what it is not. Right?

Keeping that in mind you can go deeper with the tactic of day dreaming and pinpoint within life coaching a success strategy for personal development and goal achievement. It's an emotional event that happens when the right questioning technique is used. That technique is the '6 Step Coaching Model'.

Also, it's always about action, yes, action which is a huge piece that includes elements of thinking, and by that, I mean thinking positively or as I tell my clients it's about day dreaming, like playing a movie of what life could be and getting emotionally involved in what you want. This tactic is part of the bridge building process I created to strengthen the goal achievement process. I teach in depth the bridge building technique in my '6 Step Coaching Model' Professional Life Coaching certification course, it's a tool that clients love to work with as they learn to make their own day dreaming movie.

DAY DREAMING

Day dreaming is a powerful tactic to bring about the manifestation of what you would really love to have in your life. I practice day dreaming every day, in fact I remember being told off in school countless times about day dreaming. If only the teacher had known that this simple act would in fact become a very strong part of my life coaching business tool kit.

I find the day dreaming process is an effective way to feed my soul, my imagination and keeps my motivation level set to high. Quite simply I take a little time, just a few minutes several times a day to imagine what I want and become emotionally connected with the idea of 'what if…' This simply roots the vision deep into my subconscious mind. As a result, I find that my thoughts for the day are top of mind about my vision, and my actions are all directed towards that daydream.

The tactic works as if by magic, but of course it requires an investment of time and a belief that anything is possible. It's a science based process proven to work by repetition of thoughts that switches on the RAS, reticular activating system in the brain.

* * * * *

All Things Are Possible … when you commit to do whatever, you possibly can, then review, possibility will continue in your life until you reach your goal. Possible is possible, think and take action.

Quote from 'Pepper Your Life with Dreams'

CONCLUSION

You don't have to waste countless hours thinking if a career in life coaching is for you.

I believe the six questions that I referred to at the beginning are the crux of your principal questions, *"Can I become a life coach and build a business, make money and enjoy time and money freedom living the dream?"* So, as I mentioned before the six questions that I referred to at the beginning of the book I believe I've answered them throughout the book. I'll write those questions and the fundamental answers again for you here.

<u>*"How can I coach professionally?"*</u>

Simply by always remaining at the coaching process as you coach. This is a technique that can be learned. To do that and enable you to support your clients as you provide world class coaching, I'd recommend you adopt the '6 Step Coaching Model' to use when working with clients to guarantee the clients move forward and that you always remain at process, that way you won't take on any stressing factors.

"Can I make money as a life coach?"

Absolutely you can and I know this for a fact as I and my life coaching students have learned to earn multiple figures in our coaching business entities. Keep in mind you are the only person to choose how much you earn. The amount you earn is up to you, as I always say, "anything is possible when you have the tools to do so". I have those tools and I can teach you which tools and how to use them for your lifestyle and business competitive advantage.

For instance you'll begin by getting clear on your vision, then setting that vision into a business plan that gives you the lifestyle you dream of. You'll follow through with the right actions step-by-step turning your dream into a reality.

"What skills do I need to coach and not become overwhelmed myself?"

There are several skills a professional life coach needs to adopt when working with clients. The first is confidentiality. Clients approach life coaches with their problems, sometimes their secrets, that's why it is paramount from the outset that you understand the legalities of confidentiality. Your discretion plays a superior role in deciding if you could work with a client. Of course, should the client share sensitive information with you that compromises your ethics and the law you will need to cease coaching immediately and consider your legal obligations. This is your call.

Being an effective life coach draws on several skills one of which is communication skills. Within your business plan and marketing materials you would have set out your coaching operating system, fees and terms and conditions. However, within your coaching sessions you will be required to actively listen to your clients' responses to your quality coaching questions, ideally based on the 6 Step Coaching Model. Using this model will allow you to dig deep within the client's mind without personal curiosity or judgement and have the client respond in an insightful clear manner.

"Do I work part-time or full-time as a life coach?"

The decision will be yours to make, but you could trial and begin part-time working into full-time hours if appropriate because you might find that your part-time coaching income more than meets your financial needs and personal wants and decide that part-time life coaching suits you better. Within the course we will pinpoint your 'freedom figure' so you know at all times the amount of working hours best suits your needs.

Currently as I write this book in September 2023 there are no regulatory requirements for life coaching. All certification offered is from independent companies providing certification in their model, system, software, or franchise operation. We offer certification to students who complete our training in the application of using the '6 Step Coaching Model'. The course is set out as a comprehensive life coaching training including niche differentiation, coaching style and set up, mindset, multiple income streams and the application of the 6SCM, providing certification at the conclusion of the course as proficiency in the application of the '6 Step Coaching Model' and includes business building techniques and client attraction strategies.

* * * * *

WHAT IS THE 6 STEP COACHING MODEL?

Throughout this book I've mentioned day-dreaming, positive forward moving steps and daily application to make steady and timely progress towards the desired goal. It takes effort to reach success, but it's possible and the 6 Step Coaching Model guarantees professional life coaches the elixir to results.

All you have to do to ensure you are a successful life coach who gets results for clients as you enjoy a lucrative work life balance is to use the power of the **6 Step Coaching Model** to both design your coaching business attracting an endless stream of hungry clients eager to work with you, and utilise the 6SCM with clients to help them recognise what they want, what is involved for them to manifest their wants using their knowledge, skills-set and current situation to develop a doable daily plan of action to move forward to achieve those desired objectives.

The 6SCM is a proven structured framework step-by-step combining personal development, mindset, science and NLP encouraging and highlighting the importance of raising vibrational energy, nurturing personal growth, boosting self-confidence, taking control of their decisions, pinpointing their purpose and taking positive forward moving action. Life coaches are enabled to gently, but firmly guide their clients to understand their true objectives, where and why they want a different future, what it means for them to achieve a certain goal and the best route to take towards turning those desires into the success they envision for themselves.

Use of the 6SCM simply delivers specific, measurable results and purposefully feeds clients with momentum and inspires them to remain focused, to align their thoughts to the goal, to measure the progress made and where necessary move the goal posts or to take a leap of faith. To stay disciplined to take daily forward moving steps forward to stay on course and achieve the success they deserve to the effort, determination, and purposeful steps they put in.

<u>*"Is life coaching a real job?"*</u>

Yes, life coaching is a real job, a job with a difference as a large number of coaches decide to work independently, rather than be part of a corporation or coaching franchise, instead they choose to work independently as a business owner proving a coaching service, thereby making their own 'job' role and keeping all of the money they bring in.

Professional life coaching deploys a progressive technique that guides the client to think outside of the box that leads to positive forward moving action.

MUSINGS

Life coaching is a wonderful occupation as it's truly the perfect opportunity to help others with their challenges and frustrations and empower them in the process. Life coaching is a service that improves human kind.

I remember the satisfaction I felt (I still do today), when I began coaching hard working clients to succeed and stay ahead of the curve enjoying a work life balance. Sharing the nuances of the 6SCM with them to gain insights to their entrepreneurial career, also to find and implement innovative strategies to navigate the opportunities, even the challenges that pop up as they build their dream lifestyle and a business they love.

Empowering clients to reach their full potential is the best way to blossom and empower yourself. You see, by helping others you help yourself. It stands to reason the Law of Reciprocity comes into play (I teach deeper on the Laws of the Universe in the Professional Life Coaching Certification course).

Getting paid while you help others is so much more than a bonus, it's a privilege to get paid as you build a successful enterprise from its beginnings to a six, seven and more figure business. Being in the business of providing professional life coaching services is not only a great occupation it's a vehicle to create substantial income and build personal relationships.

Another additional bonus is the gradual development of self-confidence that automatically happens and filters into all areas of your life as you work at being your own boss with the autonomy of setting in motion flexible work and play time schedule, the ability to preferred travel and money freedom factors built in. Believe me life coaching is a real opportunity to determine your own success path and living a life by design. I encourage you to consider becoming a professional life coach.

OTHER BOOKS BY PATRISHA-ANNE TODD

These books are available for purchase on Amazon worldwide.

Some of the books are stand alone, others are in a series and some books have accompanying workbooks and courses.

You can click the link below to see which books are current on the worldwide Amazon sites.

https://www.amazon.com/author/patrisha-anne

- ☐ Pepper Your Life with Dreams – 365 motivational quotes
- ☐ The Pepper Your Life with Dreams Journal
- ☐
- ☐ 7 Powerful Steps To Success

☐ 7 Powerful Steps To Success Workbook – [Q2/2024]

☐

☐ 6 Step Coaching Model

☐

☐ Life Coaching A-Z series – [Q2/2024]

☐

☐ The Business Plan for Guaranteed Success – [Q2/2024]

☐

☐ 33 Income Streams Skyrocket Your Business – [Q2/2024]

Just so you know, you can keep up to date with the new books being published, the courses offered and offers currently running.

Please visit the coaching hub @

CoachingLeadsToSuccess.com

While you are there you can claim a gift I have waiting for you.

ABOUT THE AUTHOR

PaTrisha-Anne Todd is an International Amazon Bestseller, an IPPY award winner, NLP Master, and founder of the life coaching hub @ 'CoachingLeadsToSuccess.com'.

Life Coaches around the world have adopted her **'6 Step Coaching Model'** to help them lead within their coaching community moving their clients forward from where they are to bridge the gap to where they want to be.

The **'6 Step Coaching Model'** book is one of several books in the series 'Life Coaching A-Z'. This book is part of the curriculum PaTrisha-Anne uses to teach her Professional Life Coaching certification students in the powerful skillset of positive forward-moving coaching and how to build a +6 figure coaching business.

'P.A.T.s.' is her signature personal development growth tool used with 1:1 clients, the Private Circle (a mastermind), and the on-line courses.

- ☐ *'Step Into Your Personal Power'* to capture and nurture a positive mental attitude to living an extraordinary life.
- ☐ *'Pepper Your Life with Dreams Vision Board'* a unique training to envision the vison. a virtual experience to begin a powerful transformation to living the dream!

'Pepper Your Life with Dreams', is book one in the personal development series filled to the brim with 365 quotes to stimulate the core belief system for personal success. There is a 30-day accompanying *'Pepper Your Life with Dreams' Journal* and the unique Vision Board course.

Her books for entrepreneurs, *'Life and Business by Design'* series introduces '*7 powerful Steps To Success*', helping to build a solid foundation to creating a lifestyle by design. You can use the '**7 Powerful Steps To Success**' as a blueprint and support in your entrepreneurial journey toward achieving your heart's desire to build a satisfying lifestyle by design. There is a workbook and on-line course *'Step Into Your Personal Power'*.

Her personal and business development books and courses are studied by creative souls from around the world.

She believes you are never to young to begin the journey into personal development, and for that reason also writes children's short stories which all contain her message of a positive attitude no matter what life throws at you, especially as every day she manages a chronic lung condition remnant of The Great London Smog of 1952, mobility challenges and is a recent cancer survivor. She has written thousands of motivational articles and given key notes on entrepreneurship, life coaching and living the dream to global audiences.

Between carrying out research for her writing projects, she explores this wonderous and exciting planet, enjoys a grown-up debate on current affairs, listens to Latin American music and savours the delights of good food and fine wine.
She lives on the south coast of England with her family and pets.

You can tap into her style of PMA positive mental attitude by visiting her online hub @ CoachingLeadsToSuccess.com

MY APPRECIATION and THANKS

It was my parents who instilled into me the idea of using the power of a PMA – positive mental attitude.

Thankfully I did as they suggested and adopted their thinking which over the years has been my constant companion, and continues to be so, to serve me well. Thank you.

Life and business coaches have been a part of my adult life and I thank each, and every one of them who throughout the years coached me towards my success. Thank you.

and remember

‘*Coaching*

Leads To Success’

A GIFT FOR YOU

I wrote this book for people like you to find out a little about the craft of professional life coaching, and I'm sure you've enjoyed reading the pages. Now, I'd like to invite you to dip a little deeper into my style of coaching, you can do that by visiting my online hub @

CoachingLeadsToSuccess.com

* * * * *